Front Cover: *Hazel* with Honeysuckle.

Back Cover: *Athene* with Harlequin.

Frontispiece: *Paloma* and *Oriole* with Ruff.

Title Page: *Melanitta.*

In A Miniature Garden

by Magdalena Byfield

Published By   HOBBY HOUSE PRESS, INC.
Cumberland, Maryland 21502

ISBN: 0-87588-175-0

TABLE OF CONTENTS

Color Illustration 3. White bisque garden statue with topiary bushes from the English garden set.

Color Illustration 4. The painted wooden sun dial.

Color Illustration 5. The Nailsea glass fountain and circular loofah and plaster flower border.

Color Illustration 6. *Garnet* pulled by Peridot.

Foreword

This book is about a collection of miniature dolls dating between 1865 and 1930 contained *not* in a dolls' house but in a *dolls' garden*. There can be few people who are not attracted by miniatures of all kinds; even the most mundane objects take on a surpassing charm when scaled down to a diminutive size. Dolls' house dolls are certainly no exception and when seen against a background of their time arranged with trappings to scale, they evoke an acute sense of wonder at the perfection of their size and their reflection of the orderly and predictable society that produced them and from which we have now moved so far. They remain for us frozen in a small world where time stands reassuringly still.

M.B.

Illustration 2. "Come and meet the family."

In A Miniature Garden

This unique miniature garden is formed basically of two separate commercially manufactured toy gardens, one of the 19th century and the other early 20th century. The 19th century set is German (probably from the Ore Mountain district) and comprises arbours, herbacious borders, (shaped in crescents, circles and strips) a mirror glass pond with applied paper water lilies, flowering shrubs, hedges, trees, potted plants and a sun dial.

The substances used in the production of this toy set are partly natural. Dyed loofah forms the greenery and the blossom is supplied by coloured plaster hundreds-and-thousands. The fruit on some of the trees is painted and varnished plaster while the branches of the trees and shrubs are in some cases natural twigs and in others, twisted wire bound with tape. The trees rest in plaster stands shaped as circular earth mounds and other items are mounted on wooden bases. A particularly charming feature is a bird's nest intricately woven of dried grass and containing two eggs discretely tucked into a rose arbour. A clematis plant "climbs" the sun dial and is of wired millinery flowers. There is also in this set a garden bench of wood and natural twigs and a birch broom.

The condition of this toy, considering the fragility of loofah, plaster and small twigs was surprisingly good, but the many fragmented pieces indicated that it was incomplete. After some repairs, it was displayed on a small coffee table. Almost immediately after the purchase of this first garden, a second one turned up. This was an early 20th century English set (probably by Brittains) comprised of box and high hedges and topiary worked bushes of pre-coloured foam rubber on wooden bases. It was, unlike the first set, in mint order and is probably complete. Herbacious borders and potted plants are millinery flowers fixed in wooden earth beds and turned wooden pots. There is also a small rockery of natural stones and dried grasses. The original greenhouse that came with this latter garden has been replaced by an Edwardian model conservatory with stained glass upper windows, an effect achieved by the adhesion of fine celluloid patterned sheets to the back of clear glass.

Although of a very different concept, the later garden integrated successfully with the first, being of the same scale and a good colour match. The whole combined so well that they were merged to represent one formal country garden. This now required something more than the space of a coffee table and a board was cut to size, covered with green velvet and inserted into a purpose built showcase which is lined with a coloured photographic backdrop of trees, the whole measuring 5 ft. (152.4cm) long, 2ft. (60.9cm) high and 20in. (50.8cm) deep.

The conservatory now houses all of the potted shrubs and fruit trees from the German set and flowering pot plants from the English. The grape vine strung under the roof (which lifts off) is millinery leaves and fruit clusters of purple glass.

Items added over the years piecemeal are as follows: a tin cold frame containing Vienna bronze potted plants; a variety of garden tools; a tin wheelbarrow now containing cabbages, cauliflowers and a cucumber; two

Color Illustration 7. *Basil* with
Meddick and Snowdrop.

Color Illustration 8. *Martin.*

2

Color Illustration 9. Nurse *Coral* and baby *Beryl* with Amber.

wickerwork garden chairs; a metal garden table and chairs, (table laid with painted and varnished paper cups and saucers and a metal tray with a cold drinks set and various fruits); a tea trolley carrying a service of Bristol glass cups and saucers and a metal teapot; a green bisque watering can; a brass water pump; classic statuary of terracotta, bisque and bronze; a bird table made in Czechoslovakia during World War II; a penny-farthing bicycle; a bench of white painted lead; a velvet sewing box on metal legs containing needlework and knitting items; a toy vintage car (infact, a tape measure); a cactus plant made in Mexico of green twill-covered paper; a wooden ladder; two sacks (compost?); five perambulators; a quantity of ivory toys and games, notably a croquet set; a painted wood dovecote; a wooden cricket set with stumps, wicket and a string bag containing cricket balls; a flocked papier mâché pony; two skin-covered ponies; a wooden and basketwork cart; seven different species of birds made of bronze, lead, glass and wood; ten breeds of dogs; four cats; a guinea pig; a bisque monkey; a metal swing; a glass fountain; wild animals (all Vienna bronzes); on a very small scale, numerous children's toys of bronze, tin, lead, wood, papier mâché, ivory, rubber and glass; several tiny woven baskets and a painted plaster toadstool.

The toadstool is situated in what is known as Crazy Corner where frogs sing from sheet music, cats play golf (these are characters based on the drawings of Louis Wain) and a monkey and Pug dog presented as sandwich-board men wish you a Merry Christmas in front and a Happy New Year behind. A mouse in a crinoline carries a shopping basket. Here also is a group of rabbits so tiny that a magnifying glass is required to inspect them properly. There is also a pair of metal spectacles with green celluloid lenses and their case on which is written "Love is Blind."

Last, but not least, are the dolls' house dolls from whom this setting was created — thirty-eight in all, not counting the miniscule dolls serving as toys to the child dolls. There are five papa dolls, six mama dolls, three nannies, a housekeeper, footman, pageboy, gardener and twenty-two children. There are, in addition, three bisque figurines (all damaged) which have been dressed in fabric clothing. One supposes that they percolated to nursery level after being broken where they must have found ready acceptance, being of a suitable scale and having the same type molded hairstyles as traditional dolls' house dolls. All of the items are more or less to the scale of one inch to one foot.

The dolls were collected together over a considerable period, coming singly or in groups. The garden items determined what period would be most appropriate and being 19th and early 20th century respectively, the 1890s seemed a suitable compromise. This was finally settled by the arrival of a man doll with a Union Jack badge on his coat lapel, suggesting Queen Victoria's Diamond Jubilee (celebrated June 22, 1897). The dolls are probably all German in origin and mostly of the bisque shoulder head type on cloth bodies. Some of the children are all-bisques and some are Frozen Charlottes. Many of the dolls wear their original clothing; some have had their garments restored or added to and some came unclothed and are completely re-dressed.

The project of keeping all of the items to the closing years of the 19th century proved difficult, due in part to the many gifts received for inclusion in the scene and my personal attachment to some objects of both earlier and later periods. For instance, one of the children's toys on the wooden bench is a miniscule Vienna bronze depicting Emily Pankhurst carrying a bag with the words "Votes for Women" painted on the front. This figure must date after 1907. Two all-bisque girl dolls date to the 1930s. Several of the items are known to have been purchased originally in the 1880s and two mama dolls probably date in the late 1860s.

In due course it seemed expedient to work out the relationships between the dolls, a fact brought about by many very reasonable questions from visiting children who invariably wanted to know "who were whose parents" and "who owned which pets" and so on. So the dolls were divided into related family groups and given dates of "birth" in readiness for the enquiring juveniles. To help memorize the names of such a large number, they were categorised into gemstones, flowers and birds. Hence, with the exception of one couple and the servants, they all have the surname of Flowerstone-Bird. "Stones" have such names as *Pearl* and *Ruby*; "Flowers", *Rose, Daisy,* etc. and "Birds", *Robin, Linnet* and so on. Scientific as well as French, Italian and English bird names are used and sometimes abbreviations such as in "Buzz," the Bulldog (Buzzard). The pets are also divided into their family's groupings. (Scientific names are followed by the vernacular in brackets.)

The host and hostess of the piece are *Peregrine* and *Paloma Flowerstone-Bird.* Their eight children are represented by dolls with mohair wigs while all other dolls have molded hairstyles. Their housekeeper, gardener and children's nurse are also in the scene. There is *Peregrine's* elder brother, *Jasper* and his wife, *Emerald.* They have four children accompanied by their nurse and a pageboy. With them, too, are *Emerald's* parents, *The Reverend* and *Mrs. Bloodstone. Peregrine's* younger brother and sister-in-law are *Basil* and *Myrtle,* and they have five children and their footman with them. The youngest of the four brothers is *Martin* and his wife, *Petronia* with their five offsprings and nursemaid. Also in the scene are the Grandparents, *Hippolais* and *Nana,* parents of the four brothers. They are accompanied by their fifth and youngest child, a daughter, *Sylvia.*

The setting is a Sunday afternoon in June 1897.

Color Illustration 11. Housekeeper
Smew with Merlin and Petrel.

Color Illustration 10. *Peregrine.*

Color Illustration 12. *Marila* and the work-table.

Color Illustration 13. *Nursemaid Finch* with *Penelope* and *Prunella*.

MR. AND MRS. PEREGRINE FLOWERSTONE-BIRD AND FAMILY, SERVANTS AND PETS

Peregrine b. 1864 (Figure 4).
Paloma (Dove, Italian) b. 1866 (Figure 4).
Linnet b. 1885 (Figure 5).
Melanitta (Sea Duck) b. 1888 (Figure 6).
Marila (Scaup) b. 1889 (Figure 7).
Robin b. 1890 (Figure 8).
Rissa (Kittiwake) b. 1891 (Figure 9).
Parula (North American Warbler) b. 1892 (Figure 10).
Oriole b. 1894 (Figure 11).
Jay b. 1896 (Figure 12).
Nightingale, Nurse (Figure 12).
Smew, Housekeeper (Duck) (Figure 13).
Rook, Gardener (Figure 14).

FAMILY PETS

Scottish Terrier .... Swift (Figure 7).
Tibetan Spaniel .... Ruff (Wader) (Figure 4).
Bulldog........................ Buzz (Buzzard) (Figure 4).
Miniature Pinscher .... Caspian (Tern) (Figure 5).
Pug................................. Merlin (Figure 7).
Guinea Pig .... Harlequin (Duck) (Figure 44).
Tortoise .... Tourterelle (Turtle Dove, French) (Figure 44).
Fawn .... Velvet (Scoter Duck) (Figure 53).
Peacock .... Capercaille (Game Bird) (Figure 53).
Owl .... Tawny (Figure 53).
Tabby Cats .... Puffin, Pippit and Petrel (Figures 7 and 11).
Black Kitten .... Pintail (Duck) (Figure 5).

Illustration 3.   The far left corner
of the garden.

The doll representing *Peregrine* (Illustration 4) is a 5½in. (13.9cm) tinted bisque shoulder head man doll with brown painted eyes and black molded hair with moustache. He has white bisque lower limbs, the legs having black mid-calf boots with raised heels. The pink cloth body has wired upper arms. The doll wears a high collared linen shirt beneath a black belted tunic. His bow tie is red and trousers are brown and white checked wool. The watch chain and belt buckle are of cut steel beads. He is shown with two cricket bats in the right hand and a string bag containing cricket balls, as well as wicket and stumps in the left. The perfectionist quality of these miniature wooden toys suggests an earlier date than the doll "carrying" them. Brown painted eyes are a feature confined to men dolls' house dolls *only* appearing first after 1885 and always combined with black hair. The matt bisque and high gloss black hair make a striking contrast and two models were made, a more rarely found version having a downturned moustache and resplendent beard. Period: (*Peregrine*) Late 19th/early 20th century.

The doll representing *Paloma* (Illustration 4) is a 5in. (12.7cm) tinted bisque shoulder head lady doll with blonde molded hair styled in the fashion

Illustration 4. *Paloma* and *Peregrine,* 5in. (12.7cm) and 5½in. (13.9cm) bisque shoulder head dolls with painted Vienna bronze dogs.

10

Illustration 5. *Linnet,* 4¼in. (10.8cm) bisque shoulder head doll with wig holding rubber "toy dolls." Rabbit, lizard, dog and kitten are painted Vienna bronzes.

for evening wear of the 1890s. Her head has painted features and her lower limbs are white bisque, the legs with black ankle boots and raised heels. The pink cloth body has wired upper arms. The doll is thought to be wearing a maternity dress though extra padding has been added to exaggerate the style. The original pink cotton wool padding was at first suspected of having slipped down but on close examination, it was found impossible to pass the wadding up through the high waistline. Therefore, it is concluded that the doll represents an expectant mother. The dress is two tones of blue silk with a lace overskirt, and the doll "carries" a straw-work fan in the left hand. The couple are illustrated with their dogs, Ruff, a Tibetan Spaniel and Buzz, the Bulldog. Both are Vienna bronzes. Period: (*Paloma*) Late 19th/early 20th century.

The doll representing twelve year old *Linnet* (Illustration 5) is a 4¼in. (10.8cm) tinted bisque shoulder head girl doll with a solid ball head and blonde mohair wig mounted on a gauze cap. The style is centre parted and dressed in a chignon but was originally in two braids falling to the front.

11

Illustration 6. *Melanitta,* 2¾in. (5.7cm) all-bisque socket head doll with wig. Pram is painted lead and contains papier mâché swaddled baby doll. Snail is a painted Vienna bronze.

Illustration 7. *Marila,* 2¾in. (6.9cm) all-bisque socket head doll with wig. Dogs and cats are Vienna bronzes.

Illustration 8. *Robin,* 2¾in. (6.9cm) all-bisque socket head doll with wig. Toy car is a novelty metal tape measure. Seated rabbit is a Vienna bronze.

The complexion coat is pale with delicately rouged cheeks and good feature painting. Her body is white cloth with untinted bisque lower limbs, the legs having boots pointed at the top in front and raised heels. The doll wears a blue-green silk blouse with matching velvet skirt and jacket and a metal clasp at the waist. She "holds" a pair of 1½in. (3.7cm) rubber "toy dolls" of the 1920s period dressed in cotton crochet outfits, representing a boy and girl; both have molded boyish hairstyles and are from identical molds. The detail in these minute dolls is remarkable with their clearly defined fingers and toes, crisp features and well modelled ears. Only the eyes are painted, and the rubber is toffee coloured rather than the usual pink. Their outfits are probably commercially made, and they are strung together with a matching crochet cord in the back. *Linnet* is shown with two of the family pets, Caspian, a Miniature Pinscher (Vienna bronze) and the black kitten, Pintail (lead with wire whiskers). Also illustrated are a Vienna bronze lizard and baby rabbit. Period: (*Linnet*) 1885-95.

The doll representing nine year old *Melanitta* (Illustration 6) is a 2¾in. (6.9cm) all-bisque girl doll peg-strung to the shoulders and hips with a bell-loop socket neck. The ball-head has finely detailed feature painting and a blonde mohair wig. Head, body and limbs are lightly tinted, the legs with blue painted boots. She is dressed in a blue and tan silk low-waisted dress with matching blue bows at the hips and in the back. Her bonnet is crocheted cotton threaded with blue ribbons. Although this model was mass-produced over a long period, the quality and dress style of this doll suggests she was one of the first. She is illustrated with a white painted lead

13

pram containing a mid-19th century papier mâché swaddled baby doll. The snail at her feet is a painted Vienna bronze. Period: (*Melanitta*) Late 19th/early 20th century.

The doll representing eight year old *Marila* (Illustration 7) is another 2¾in. (6.9cm) all-bisque girl doll, identical in size and mold to Illustration 6 except for the wig style which is straight with a fringe and is applied direct to the head without a cap. She probably dates to the 1890s, but her dress was crocheted in 1947 by a Slovakian needlewoman. The writer watched fascinated while it was made within an hour from a single reel of white cotton with a hook so fine, when it once fell to the carpet, it was difficult to locate! The doll is shown with Scottish Terrier, Swift, cats, Pippit and Petrel and Pug dog, Merlin. All are painted Vienna bronzes. Period: (*Marila*) Late 19th/early 20th century.

The doll representing seven year old *Robin* (Illustration 8) is a 2¾in. (6.9cm) all-bisque boy doll from the same mold as the two previous dolls, but possibly of a later period. The complexion coat is warmer and the feature painting, while extremely slick, is not of the same high standard. The wig, too, is the later type associated with all-bisques of this diminutive size, being a continuous roll of curled brown mohair glued to the head until the entire area was covered. He is dressed in a suit made of red and white cotton edging with a blue silk sash. Shown with the doll is a metal car with white rubber tyres from which a tape measure on a spring can be drawn from

Illustration 9. *Rissa,* 2¾in. (6.9cm) all-bisque socket head doll with wig. Surrounded by toys of ivory, wood, bisque and bronze. Rustic bench is from the German garden set.

the back. Seated in the car is a painted Vienna bronze depicting the Beatrix Potter character, Benjamin Bunny. Period: (*Robin*) Late 19th/early 20th century.

The doll representing six year old *Rissa* (Illustration 9) is again a 2¾in. (6.9cm) all-bisque of the same mold as the previous dolls but with outstandingly detailed features. The centre parted long black mohair wig shows signs of having once been plaited. The high gloss colouring used for the eyes is so lustrous that the doll was sold as a glass-eyed specimen. She is dressed in a golden brown silk blouse and skirt with a dark brown silk hat. Her boots are painted red (the previous three specimens having blue boots). This doll is photographed seated on a rustic bench from the German garden set, surrounded by toys of ivory, bisque, wood and Vienna bronze. Period: (*Rissa*) Late 19th/early 20th century.

The doll representing five year old *Parula* (Illustration 10) is a 2¼in. (5.7cm) parian-type Frozen Charlotte with painted features, a ball head with long light brown mohair wig mounted on a gauze cap and tied back at the nape of the neck. From the knees down the legs are glazed and decorated with grape lustre mid-calf bands and ankle boots. She wears a light green silk dress which is low-waisted, trimmed with shirred ribbon at the hem, and decorated at the waist with silk flowers and bowknots. This doll is illustrated with a wood and metal pram and a carriage containing three rabbits. Period: (*Parula*) 1880-90.

Illustration 10. *Parula,* 2¼in. (5.7cm) bisque Frozen Charlotte with wig and lustre boots. Toys are painted wood and lead.

Illustration 11. *Oriole,* 2¾in. (6.9cm) all-bisque socket head doll seated in metal swing. Cat and mouse are painted Vienna bronzes.

The doll representing three year old *Oriole* (Illustration 11) is another 2¾in. (6.9cm) all-bisque with a bell-loop socket neck, painted features and the remains of a blonde mohair wig beneath her lace cap. She is dressed in a cotton print frock with lace overskirt and pink silk sash tied in a bow at the back. Her boots are painted red. She is shown seated in a metal swing with Puffin, the cat chasing a mouse. Both animals are painted Vienna bronzes. Period: (*Oriole*) Late 19th/early 20th century.

The doll representing one year old *Jay* (Illustration 12) is a 1¼in. (3.1cm) all-bisque child doll, the head and body molded in one with wire-strung articulation at the shoulders and hips. The ball head has a blonde mohair wig without a cap, and the close-set painted eyes suggest either a French origin or that the model was destined for the French market. The complexion coat is pale but patchy. The legs are modelled with molded boots and ribbed hose which have been left unpainted. The doll is elaborately dressed in a peach silk baby robe trimmed with shirred ribbon at the hem. A lawn bonnet ties beneath the chin and is decorated with rouched pink silk. The cape is gold embroidered burgundy velvet trimmed with shirred ribbon; a wide collar of embroidered lawn fastens at the neck with a large pink bowknot. Period: (*Jay*) 1885-95.

The doll representing *Nightingale,* the children's nurse (Illustration 12) is a 5in. (12.7cm) bisque shoulder head lady doll with a fresh complexion coat, painted features and light brown molded hairstyle. Her body is pink cloth with wired upper arms. She has white bisque lower limbs, the legs

Illustration 12. *Nurse Nightingale,* 5in. (12.7cm) bisque shoulder head doll holding *Jay,* the baby, a 1¼in. (3.1cm) all-bisque doll with wig.

wearing black court shoes. This doll is dressed in a grey and white herring-bone rib cotton frock with lace trimmed starched lawn apron and cap which ties beneath the chin with silk ribbons. Her charge is tied to her left arm with ribbons attached to the back of the baby's cape, and in the right hand she "holds" a group of three papier mâché toy dolls from a Pedlar's pack. Period: (*Nightingale*) Late 19th/early 20th century.

The doll representing *Smew*, the housekeeper (Illustration 13) is a 5in. (12.7cm) lightly tinted bisque shoulder head lady doll with painted features and dark blonde molded hairdo. Her body is pink cloth with wired upper arms and her lower limbs are white bisque, the legs having molded black one-strap court shoes. She is dressed in a black linen frock with a white collar and cuffs and a lace-trimmed cotton apron. Four metal keys on a ring are suspended on a black ribbon from a cut steel clasp at the corsage which is padded. As with many factory dressed dolls' house dolls, the skirt

Illustration 13. *Smew,* the housekeeper, 5in. (12.7cm) bisque shoulder head doll with metal tea trolley.

is lined with white gauze. The doll is shown beside a gilt metal trolley laid with a Bristol glass tea service and metal teapot. Period: (*Smew*) Late 19th/early 20th century.

Illustration 14. *Rook,* the gardener, 6in. (15.2cm) bisque shoulder head doll holding birch broom and garden fork. Shown beside a wired loofah pear tree with painted plaster fruit.

The doll representing *Rook,* the gardener (Illustration 14) is a 6in. (15.2cm) tinted bisque shoulder head man doll with molded dark brown hair, moustache and beard. His body is unbleached cloth with lower limbs of white bisque, the legs having small black pointed ankle boots and slightly raised heels. He is dressed in a white cotton shirt with an open collar; the sleeves (with rolled cuffs) are attached to the upper arms and not the shirt. A red and white neckerchief is loosely tied at the throat. The belt and apron are leather and worn over blue cotton trousers tied with cord below the knees. The trouser legs are separate and stitched to the body at the waist. The outfit is extremely faded and fragile and suggests the doll was professionally dressed, possibly in representation of a blacksmith. It is illustrated with a pear tree and birch broom from the German garden and a wood and metal fork "held" in the left hand. Period: (*Rook*) 1885-1900.

Illustration 15. Painted tin cold frame containing Vienna bronze pot plants. Watering can is green bisque and metal sun-glasses have green celluloid lenses. Sacks are sawdust filled coarse cloth. Lid is propped with wood and metal garden fork and robin on top is a Vienna bronze.

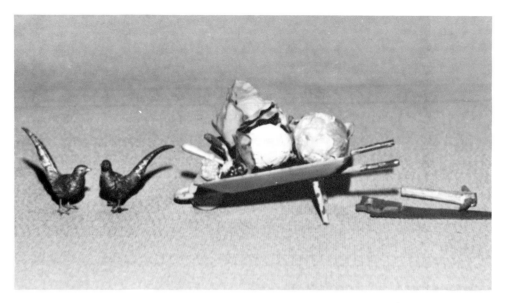

Illustration 16. Metal wheelbarrow laden with vegetables of painted plaster and copper. Pheasants are Vienna bronzes and tools at right are of metal and wood.

Illustration 17. Mirror glass lily pond with applied paper water lillies. Nymph statuette is a bronze seal and water pump is brass. Carved wooden Chinese fishing birds have metal legs.

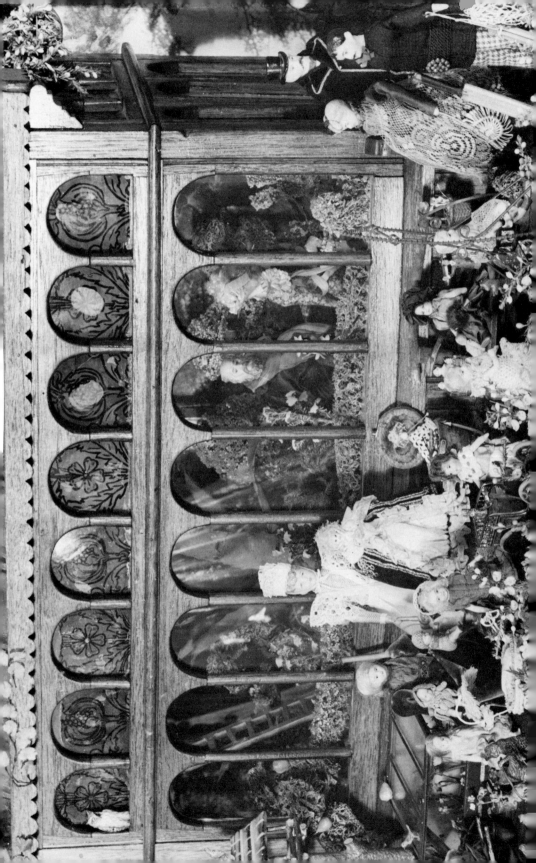

MR. AND MRS. JASPER FLOWERSTONE-BIRD AND FAMILY, SERVANTS AND PETS

Jasper b. 1862 (Figures 19 and 22).
Emerald b. 1872 (Figures 19 and 21).
Ruby and *Pearl* b. 1891 (Figures 20 and 23).
Garnet b. 1894 (Figures 20 and 24).
Beryl b. 1896 (Figures 20 and 25).
Coral, Nurse (Figures 20 and 25).
Spinel, Pageboy (Figure 24).
The Reverend Bloodstone (Figures 26 and 29).

Parents of Emerald.

Mrs. Bloodstone (Figures 26 and 29).

PETS

Pony . . . . Tourmaline (Figures 19 and 21).
Great Danes . . . . Corundum and Crystal (Figures 19 and 21).
Greyhound . . . . Peridot (Figure 24).
Airedale . . . . Amber (Figures 20 and 25).
Monkey . . . . Jewel (Figure 26).

Illustration 18.   The centre left of the garden.

The doll representing *Jasper* (Illustrations 19 and 22) is a 6in. (15.2cm) bisque shoulder head man doll with light blonde molded hair and moustache. He has a pale complexion coat and finely painted features. His lower limbs are white bisque, the legs wearing ankle boots and raised heels. The body and upper limbs are white cloth. He is dressed in a blue and grey striped sporting outfit and fabric leggings and is shown with a metal Penny-Farthing bicycle with a leather saddle. Period: (*Jasper*) 1885-95.

The doll representing *Emerald* (Illustrations 19 and 21) is a 6in. (15.2cm) parian-type bisque shoulder head lady doll with a light blonde molded hairstyle decorated in front with blue and gold lustre ornaments and in back with a lustre comb. Her molded drop earrings are also gold lustre. She has outstandingly well painted features and white bisque lower limbs, the legs wearing flat black ankle boots. The body is unbleached linen. This doll wears a green silk outfit with a braid trimmed blue collar reinforced on the reverse with paper backing. Her matching green hat has a dark blue feather plume and a green ribbon bow. She "carries" a canework riding crop and has been arranged to sit side saddle on a wood and papier mâché pony. This flocked dapple grey was a sweet container of the 1880s; the head pulls off at the base of the neck. She is photographed with a pair of

Illustration 19. *Emerald* and *Jasper*, 6in. (15.2cm) bisque shoulder head dolls.

Illustration 20. *Nurse Coral* with her four charges and pet Airedale.

Vienna bronze Great Danes. The doll has the rare distinction of having a wardrobe and accessories (Illustrations 27 and 28). Period: (*Emerald*) 1865-75. This model is also found in larger sizes.

The dolls representing six year old *Ruby* and *Pearl* (Illustrations 20 and 23) are 2¾in. (6.9cm) bisque shoulder head girl dolls with light blonde molded hairstyles, a pale complexion tint and painted features. Their lower limbs are white bisque, the legs having ribbed hose and black ankle boots with raised heels. The bodies are peach-coloured cloth. Both dolls are dressed alike in navy and white silk taffeta with lace trim and rainbow sashes. Although their heads were cast from the same mold, the variations in their excellent feature painting gives them very different expressions. Pearl "carries" her toy doll which is a 1½in. (3.7cm) all-bisque with molded boyish hairstyle, wire articulated at shoulders and hips, and dressed in knitted lace. Ruby's coloured doll in the pram is a bisque cake decoration item molded in one with a cradle which sinks into the pram and is concealed by rouched lace. The ball at their feet is black and white Venetian glass. Period: (*Ruby and Pearl*) 1880-90.

The doll representing three year old *Garnet* (Illustrations 20 and 24) is a 2½in. (6.3cm) all-bisque bent limb baby doll with metal strung articulation at shoulders and hips. He has naturalistic flesh colouring with painted features. His molded boyish hairstyle is russet brown and has deep comb marks. He wears a dress of cream satin with lace and ribbon trim. His hat is pink and blue velvet with a white plume. The doll has a woven basket over his left arm and "holds" a bunch of balloons in his right hand. These have been improvised out of celluloid mistletoe berries from a spray of artificial flowers. Some have been left their original white colour and others were dipped in strong solutions of fabric dye. They are supported on millinery wires. The cart of wood, metal, basketwork and applied paper is "drawn" by a bronze Greyhound wearing a collar of tiny strung beads. This is probably a stray from a Pedlar Doll's basket. Many small perfectionist items

Illustration 22. *Jasper,* 6in. (15.2cm) bisque shoulder head doll in cycling costume. Penny-farthing is metal with leather saddle.

Illustration 21. (Page 26) *Emerald,* a parian-type bisque shoulder head doll with lustre hair adornments and earrings. Pony was a novelty sweet box and Great Danes are bronze.

of this nature were made for the purpose of furnishing pedlars or miniature bazaars. This doll is illustrated with a pageboy holding the dog. Period: (*Garnet*) 1900-25.

The doll representing six month old *Beryl* (Illustrations 20 and 25) is a 2¼in. (5.7cm) bisque Frozen Charlotte with molded blonde hair in a boyish style with deep comb marks. It has a pale complexion coat with excellent feature painting. The doll is modelled in a semi-lying position and is dressed in a bonnet and gown and sewn into an elaborate swaddling wrapper. Her comforter is applied ivory, and the rattle is ivory and silvered glass. This type of Frozen Charlotte is associated with 19th century Easter

Illustration 23. *Ruby* and *Pearl,* 2¾in. (6.9cm) bisque shoulder head twin dolls and their toys.

gifts, being often found inside an egg container. In origin, its roots are probably religious (like the Christmas tree fairy) but by the 1880s the derivation was largely lost and they had evolved into seasonal baubles for children. The doll is shown in the arms of her nurse. Period: (*Beryl*) 1875-85.

The doll representing *Nurse Coral* (Illustrations 20 and 25) is a 5½in. (13.9cm) tinted bisque shoulder head lady doll with mid-brown molded hairstyle and painted features. She has white bisque lower limbs, the legs having black ankle boots and raised heels. Her body is pink cloth with wired upper arms. She wears a belted navy blue dress with white pleated collar and cuffs, a white apron and navy cape. The matching toque and tülle veil are

Illustration 24. *Garnet*, 2½in. (6.3cm) all-bisque doll seated in a cart drawn by a bronze Greyhound, lead by *Spinel*, the pageboy, a 4in. (12.2cm) parian-type bisque shoulder head doll.

Illustration 25. *Nurse Coral*, 5½in. (13.9cm) bisque shoulder head doll carrying *Beryl*, the baby, 2¼in. (5.7cm) bisque Frozen Charlotte. Dog is a painted Vienna bronze.

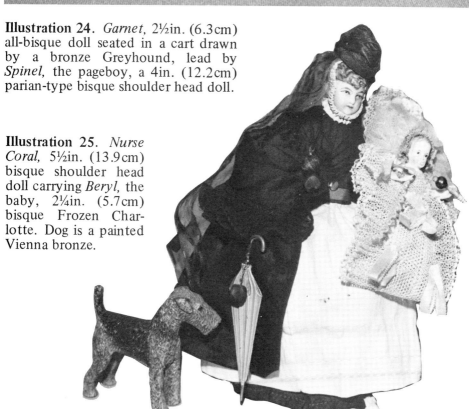

Illustration 26. *The Reverend and Mrs. Bloodstone.* He is a 6in. (15.2cm) bisque figurine wearing fabric clothing. She is a 6in. (15.2cm) bisque shoulder head doll. Pet monkey is bisque.

Illustration 27. Some of *Emerald's* dresses and accessories.

worn over a white pleated wimple. Her umbrella is, in fact, a brooch pinned to the skirt. One elegant white shoe showing at the hem is a separate item carved from a beach pebble. The Airedale is a painted Vienna bronze. This is the same model as the nursemaid doll in Illustration 12. Period: (*Coral*) Late 19th/early 20th century.

The doll representing *Spinel*, the pageboy (Illustration 24) is a 4in. (10.2cm) parian-type bisque shoulder head boy doll with molded blonde hair and well painted features. His lower limbs are white bisque, the legs having flat black ankle boots. He is commercially dressed to represent a footman in a brown felt jacket with gold braid trim and gold bead buttons. His necktie and cuffs are cotton and he has corded breeches and a waistcoat with white bead buttons. His linen leggings have gold braid at the knees. The colour of cloth body is not known as the clothes are tightly sewn to the doll. Period. (*Spinel*) 1875-85.

The figure representing *The Reverend Bloodstone* (Illustrations 26 and 29) is a Russian 6in. (15.2cm) bisque figurine depicting an elderly man made by Gardener of the Moscow Porcelain Factory. His very finely detailed head has superb brushwork decoration and delicate colouring. The body (with one arm missing) wears a long molded coat which is now concealed by a black fabric cape with an orange muslin neck scarf. Factory and sculptor's marks, also the mold number are stamped on the base of the pedestal.

Illustration 28. Another of *Emerald's* dresses and a shawl.

He is shown "holding" a pet monkey, Jewel, a finely tinted and decorated brown bisque animal. Period: (*The Reverend Bloodstone*) circa 1875.

The doll representing *Mrs. Bloodstone* (Illustrations 26 and 29) is a 6in. (15.2cm) tinted bisque shoulder head lady doll with molded hairstyle and painted features. This is the same model as the housekeeper doll in Illustration 13. She has white bisque lower limbs, the legs wearing brown molded shoes and raised heels. Her body is pink cloth with wired upper arms. She is dressed in a cotton print jacket and skirt, the latter with black velvet ribbon decoration and waistband. This doll wears a straw hat with plumes and ribbon decoration "borrowed" from her daughter's wardrobe. Her blouse is blue silk with a white collar. Period: (*Mrs. Bloodstone*) Late 19th/early 20th century.

Illustration 29. Emerald's parents, *The Reverend and Mrs. Bloodstone in* the conservatory.

ABOVE: Illustration 30. A part of the conservatory roof showing the grapevine. Dove on the outside is a painted Vienna bronze.

RIGHT: Illustration 31. The cactus plant housed inside the conservatory, made in Mexico of twill covered paper mounted on a wooden base with carved wooden painted rocks.

MR. AND MRS. BASIL FLOWERSTONE-BIRD AND FAMILY, SERVANT AND PETS

Basil b. 1866 (Figure 33).
Myrtle b. 1868 (Figures 33 and 37).
Hazel b. 1887 (Figure 34).
Florian and *Marigold* b. 1888 (Figure 35).
Rose b. 1894 (Figure 36).
Pansy b. 1896 (Figures 33 and 37).
Broom, Footman (Figure 36).

PETS

Pony . . . . Honeysuckle (Figure 34).
Foal . . . . Buttercup (Figure 34).
Black Chow . . . . Medick (Figure 33).
White Chow . . . . Snowdrop (Figure 33).
Brown Chow . . . . Poppy (Figures 33 and 37).

Illustration 32. The central area of the garden.

The doll representing *Basil* (Illustration 33) is a 5¾in. (14.5cm) tinted bisque shoulder head man doll with painted features which include grey wrinkle lines on his forehead. His molded hair with sideburns is light brown with comb marks; his deeply molded upturned moustache is of a slightly darker tone. The lower limbs are white bisque, the legs with rather large feet wearing molded knee-high black boots with square heels. He is dressed in a shirt and red tie with an embroidered linen waistcoat and black, grey and white checked trousers. His coat and artist-type cap are navy blue wool. The badge on his left lapel is a silk covered Union Jack button. This doll "holds" four miniature prints in his left hand. Period: (*Basil*) 1900-14.

The doll representing *Myrtle* (Illustrations 33 and 37) is a 5¾in. (14.5cm) parian-type bisque shoulder head lady doll with a light blonde molded upswept hairdo. She has painted features with well modelled ears pierced through and is wearing strung bead earrings. The necklace around her throat is gold paper. Her body is unbleached linen with elongated white bisque lower arms and glazed porcelain lower legs with flat black ankle boots. She is dressed in a brown silk grosgrain and velvet frock with matching hat decorated with a single feather. On her right arm the doll "holds" her baby, and in the left hand a green knitted purse with pinchbeck rings and tassels. The dolls are shown together with three Chows, namely Medick,

Illustration 33. *Basil* and *Myrtle,* both 5¾in. (14.5cm) bisque shoulder head dolls with their baby, *Pansy* and three Chows.

Snowdrop and Poppy. The white and black dogs are painted composition and the brown dog is a Vienna bronze. Period: (*Myrtle*) 1870-80. This model is also found in larger sizes.

The doll representing ten year old *Hazel* (Illustration 34) is a 3¼in. (8.2cm) tinted bisque shoulder head child doll with painted features and short light brown molded hair. She has a peg-jointed body with a wooden dowel passing up through the neck. Her lower limbs are painted but not varnished, the legs having white socks and pale grey ankle boots. She is dressed in yellow silk and wears a separate top hat trimmed with a black veil and yellow plume. The jointing method of this body type enabled the doll to be realistically arranged in a side-saddle pose. The Shetland pony, Honeysuckle and foal, Buttercup are skin covered wood with glass eyes. Their tack is leather, cord and metal. The doll "carries" a riding crop made from a pin bound with cotton thread. Period: (*Hazel*) circa 1880.

The doll representing nine year old *Florian* (Illustration 35) is a 3½in. (8.8cm) tinted bisque shoulder head boy doll with his head turned slightly to the left. He has side-glancing painted eyes and light brown molded hair

Illustration 34. *Hazel,* 3¼in. (8.2cm) bisque shoulder head doll on a peg-jointed body. Ponies are skin-covered wood.

Illustration 35. *Florian* and *Marigold*, 3½in. (8.8cm) bisque shoulder head dolls of the same mold.

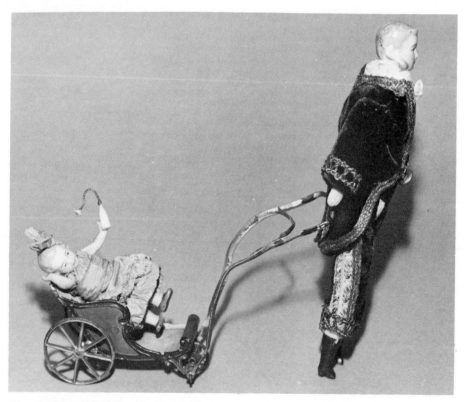

Illustration 36. *Rose*, 2¼in. (5.7cm) all-bisque doll drawn in a painted lead carriage by *Finch*, the footman, 5½in. (13.9cm) bisque shoulder head doll.

with comb marks. The body is pink cloth with wired upper arms. His lower limbs are white bisque, but in the case of this doll the legs have been over-painted to simulate black hose and blue buttoned boots with black toe caps. The upper cloth section of legs has also been tinted black. He wears a black velvet suit with a lace collar and cuffs. The left hand "holds" a metal hoop and in the right an exceptionally detailed woven-hair hat. Period: (*Florian*) Late 19th/early 20th century.

The doll representing nine year old *Marigold* (Illustration 35) is the identical model to *Florian*; the dolls are fittingly cast in the role of twins. This doll, however, is wearing original girl's clothing of rose sateen and organdie with matching bows at the waist and applied to the head. The V-shaped neckline is trimmed with lace. She "pushes" a black and red three-wheeler tin pram in which is seated a 1½in. (3.7cm) brown all-bisque doll with painted features and molded black hair, wire strung at shoulders and hips. The complexion tint has been carried over molded ribbed hose and boots. She is dressed in a red and gold outfit and red turban decorated with a gold flower-sequin. Period: (*Marigold*) Late 19th/early 20th century.

The doll representing three year old *Rose* (Illustration 36) is a 2¼in. (5.7cm) all-bisque girl doll with a blonde molded hairstyle incorporating a bisque loop for the ribbon tie. Her painted features include a smiling mouth and teeth. She has wire strung articulation at the shoulders and hips. The legs have molded ankle socks and brown slippers with slightly raised heels. Her sleeveless pink silk frock has a broad sash and lace trim on the skirt and a matching hair ribbon. Her left hand "holds" an ivory and tin

Illustration 37. Baby *Pansy,* 1½in. (3.7cm) seated bisque figurine with molded bonnet dressed in fabric. shown on the arm of her mother, *Myrtle,* 5¾in. (14.5cm) bisque shoulder head doll.

Illustration 38. Three garden statues. Left to right: bronze, terracotta and white bisque.

feeding bottle. The doll is riding in a three-wheeler lead cart painted red, blue and white and drawn by a footman. Period: (*Rose*) 1920-30.

The figure representing eighteen month old *Pansy* (Illustrations 33 and 37) is a 1½in. (3.7cm) seated bisque figurine with a blue molded bonnet. The applied rose organdie dress and pink muslin petticoat are fabrics shared by the dolls in Illustrations 35 and 43 and all three came from the same source. The plush plume conceals a chip in the bonnet. She has very detailed feature painting and comb marked hair showing in front. She is seen on the arm of her mama. Period: (*Pansy*) circa 1885.

The doll representing *Broom*, the footman (Illustration 36) is a 5½in. (13.9cm) tinted bisque shoulder head man doll with painted features and molded blonde hair and sideburns. (By the 1890s side whiskers without other facial hair denoted a menial status except in elders.) The doll's body is pink cloth with wired upper arms and white bisque lower limbs. His legs have molded black mid-calf boots with raised heels. He is dressed in brocade and dark red velvet livery trimmed with gold braid. The cravat at his neck is cream chifon. Period: (*Broom*) Late 19th/early 20th century.

40

ABOVE: Illustration 39. A view of the painted wooden dovecote beside the conservatory.

RIGHT: Illustration 40. The painted wooden sun dial with climbing plant of millinery flowers and leaves. The worktable contains knitting and needlework items.

41

MR. AND MRS. MARTIN FLOWERSTONE-BIRD AND FAMILY, SERVANT AND DOG

Martin b. 1867 (Figure 42).
Petronia (Rock Sparrow) b. 1866 (Figure 42).
Marinus (Great Black-backed Gull) b. 1887 (Figure 43).
Isabelline (Wheatear) b. 1888 (Figure 43).
Athene (Little Owl) b. 1890 (Figures 1 and 44).
Penelope (Widgeon) and *Prunella* (Sparrow) b. 1896 (Figures 45 and 46).
Finch, Nursemaid (Figure 46).

PET

Bull Terrier . . . . Wagtail (Figure 42).

Illustration 41.   The centre right
of the garden.

The doll representing *Martin* (Illustration 42) is a 5½in. (13.9cm) hatted shoulder head man doll. He is a high grade tinted bisque with painted features and blonde molded hair showing beneath his molded black top hat. His comb-marked moustache is glossy brown. He has a peach coloured cloth body with tinted bisque lower arms and white bisque lower legs with ribbed hose and mid-calf black boots. The doll is partly commercially dressed with later additions. The most unusual item of his clothing is the professionally made high collared shirt which fastens down the back with minute hooks and eyes. The cravat is blue silk. Home additions are the black felt and velvet Chesterfield jacket with braid edging and bead buttons. His trousers are dark blue wool. This doll first arrived with one leg missing (which followed later) and was initially supported on miniature wood crutches — which stuck! Period: (*Martin*) 1880-90.

The doll representing *Petronia* (Illustration 42) is a 5in. (12.7cm) tinted bisque shoulder head lady doll, identical to the mama doll in Illustration 4. Her dress is of three layers of material, spotted black net over white tülle on a foundation of black satin. Her cuffs and belt are black velvet,

Illustration 42. *Martin* and *Petronia,* 5½in. (13.9cm) and 5in. (12.7cm) bisque shoulder head dolls with painted Vienna bronze dog.

Illustration 43. *Isabeline* and *Marinus,* 3½in. (8.8cm) and 4½in. (11.4cm) bisque shoulder head dolls. Girl holds a 1½in. (3.7cm) all-bisque doll and boy carries an ivory tennis racket.

Illustration 44. *Athene,* 3¾in. (9.4cm) all-bisque girl doll playing with a painted wooden Sicilian horse. Guinea pig and tortoise are painted Vienna bronzes.

and the padded corsage is decorated with green silk ribbon bowknots. Her fabric hat is light green with two black feathers. The couple are shown with their Bull Terrier, Wagtail who is a painted Vienna bronze. Period: (*Petronia*) Late 19th/early 20th century.

The doll representing ten year old *Marinus* (Illustration 43) is a 4½in. (11.4cm) hatted boy doll, the shoulder head with molded pale blue shirt, white collar and lilac tie. His sailor-type hat is black with a molded band. His blonde hair is comb marked. He has well painted features including large black eyes on a flesh tinted complexion coat. The doll's body is unbleached linen with white bisque lower limbs, the legs with black ankle boots and raised heels. He is dressed in a blue velvet suit with two lilac buttons. This doll "carries" an ivory and string tennis racket. Period: (*Marinus*) 1880-90. This model is also found in larger sizes.

The doll representing nine year old *Isabelline* (Illustration 43) is a 3½in. (8.8cm) tinted bisque shoulder head girl doll with molded light brown hair with a black painted circlet. This is the companion doll to the models illustrated in Illustration 35. Her body is pink cloth with wired upper arms and white bisque lower limbs, the legs with almost flat black ankle boots. Her dress is lace-edged pink muslin over white silk with a cream ribbon tie at waist. Her toy doll is a 1½in. (3.7cm) parian-type all-bisque, peg strung at shoulders and hips with blonde molded hair and finely painted features. She has molded ribbed hose and boots with heels which have been left undecorated. Her commercially made dress is blue and white cotton crochet. Period: (*Isabelline*) Late 19th/early 20th century.

The doll representing seven year old *Athene* (Illustrations 1 and 44) is a 3¾in. (9.4cm) all-bisque girl doll, wire strung at shoulders and hips. She

Illustration 46. The nursemaid, *Finch,* 5½in. (13.9cm) bisque shoulder head doll carrying her twin charges.

Illustration 47. The Nailsea glass fountain with a circular floral border of loofah and painted plaster flower clusters.

Illustration 48. The ivory croquet set with a metal garden chair and loofah tree.

has finely detailed features with smiling unpainted lips. Her molded hairstyle is comb-marked and her painted features include black eyes and dark blonde eyebrows to match her hair colour. This doll has painted black stockings to above the knee with flat blue one-strap shoes. Her dress is white spotted black velvet with a white ribbon tie at the waistline. She is shown with a Sicilian toy horse of painted wood and painted bronzes of the tortoise, Tourterelle and guinea pig, Harlequin. Period: (*Athene*) 1920-30.

The heads representing one year old twins *Penelope* and *Prunella* (Illustrations 45 and 46) are bisque half-heads (or plaqueheads) glued into a padded swaddling wrapper with blue silk ribbon ties. The gathered lace around the faces conceals the join. Presented in this manner, they are thought to have been Christening favours. Their parian-type bisque heads have molded blonde hair with comb marks and painted features. Height of heads, ¼in. (.6cm). Period: (*Penelope and Prunella*) 1880-90.

The doll representing the nursemaid, *Finch* (Illustration 46) is the same model and height as the two nannie dolls in Illustrations 12 and 25. Her dress is pink wool decorated with white braid and lace trim with a cap and streamers of lace over gauze. She wears a double apron of pink and white linen with an elaborate lace apron on top. This doll is shown "holding" her swaddled twin charges. Period: (*Finch*) Late 19th/early 20th century.

Illustration 49. The wooden bird table and some garden tools. Squirrel is a painted Vienna bronze.

49

THE GRANDPARENTS,
MR. AND MRS. HIPPOLAIS FLOWERSTONE-BIRD AND DAUGHTER

Hippolais (Warbler) b. 1832 (Figure 51).
Nana (Desert Warbler) b. 1842 (Figure 51).
Sylvia (Garden Warbler) b. 1879 (Figure 52).

Illustration 50. The far right corner
of the garden.

The doll representing *Hippolais* (Illustration 51) is a 5¼in. (13.3cm) tinted bisque shoulder head grandfather doll with painted features including grey wrinkle lines, and a balding head with molded grey hair and sideburns. His body is pink cloth with wired upper arms. The lower limbs are white bisque, the legs with black ankle boots and raised heels. The doll wears a cape over a brown linen suit and a white cotton shirt with a blue bow tie. The cape is quilted green silk with a fur-fabric collar and the matching smoking cap is felt and fur-fabric with a yellow tassel. Period: (*Hippolais*) Late 19th/early 20th century.

The doll representing *Nana* (Illustration 51) is a 5¼in. (13.3cm) tinted bisque shoulder head grandmother doll with painted features including grey wrinkle lines. Her molded hairdo is painted grey. The body is pink cloth with wired upper arms. The lower limbs are white bisque, the legs having

Illustration 51. *Hippolais* and *Nana,* 5¼in. (13.3cm) bisque shoulder head dolls with painted grey hair and wrinkle lines.

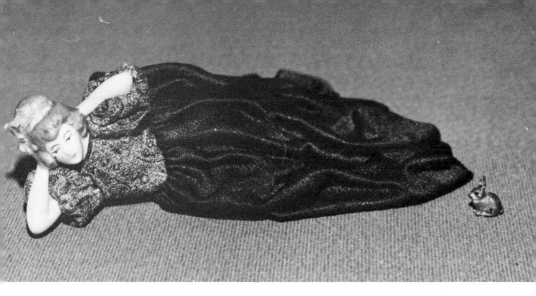

Illustration 52. *Sylvia,* 4½in. (11.4cm) reclining bisque figurine dressed in fabric blouse and skirt.

molded black ankle boots. The doll wears a black silk dress with two rows of black velvet ribbons at the hem. Her matching hat has a long tülle veil. Her umbrella is wood bound with black silk and a coral handle. Period: (*Nana*) Late 19th/early 20th century.

The reclining figure representing eighteen year old *Sylvia* (Illustration 52) is a tinted bisque figurine of the type known to collectors as Bathing Beauties, usually found nude or wearing open-work swimsuits in the Edwardian style. The figure has painted features and an elaborate blonde molded hairdo incorporating a pink ribbon and bowknot. She is dressed in a home-sewn paisley-pattern blouse and dark green sateen skirt. She measures 4½in. (11.4cm) in length and is shown with a Vienna bronze baby rabbit. Period: (*Sylvia*) 1910-20.

Illustration 53. Some Vienna bronzes from Crazy Corner.

Illustration 54. Painted Vienna bronze owl, deer and peacock.

Illustration 55. "The End."

Index